THIS
JOURNAL
BELONGS
TO

IF FOUND PLEASE
Contact

SONGWRITER'S journal

WRITTEN AND ILLUSTRATED BY
ELIZABETH EVANS

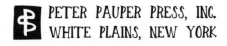

PETER PAUPER PRESS, INC.
WHITE PLAINS, NEW YORK

PETER PAUPER PRESS
Fine Books and Gifts Since 1928

Our Company

In 1928, at the age of twenty-two, Peter Beilenson began printing books on a small press in the basement of his parents' home in Larchmont, New York. Peter—and later, his wife, Edna—sought to create fine books that sold at "prices even a pauper could afford."

Today, still family owned and operated, Peter Pauper Press continues to honor our founders' legacy—and our customers' expectations—of beauty, quality, and value.

FOR DORIS AND WALTER WILEY, WHO MADE AMERICAN ROOTS MUSIC THE SOUNDTRACK OF MY CHILDHOOD.

Illustration copyright © 2014 ElizabethJEvans.com

Copyright © 2014
Peter Pauper Press, Inc.
202 Mamaroneck Avenue
White Plains, NY 10601
ISBN 978-1-4413-1413-0
Printed in China
7 6 5 4 3

Visit us at www.peterpauper.com

Table
OF
CONTENTS

Introduction

Songwriting is a personal expression for each artist. Joan Baez explains her own songwriting process as being like a channel, receiving songs from a place outside of herself: "It seems to me that those songs that have been any good, I have nothing much to do with the writing of them. The words have just crawled down my sleeve and come out on the page." For Leonard Cohen songwriting is more intentional and laborious. "I wish I were one of those people who wrote songs quickly," he says. "But I'm not. So it takes me a great deal of time to find out what the song is. I am working most of the time."

No matter how you operate or where your songs originate, it is essential as an artist to have a place to record and organize your ideas. This journal has been designed to inspire and shape creativity and to awaken your inner muse.

HOW·TO·USE THIS JOURNAL

The pages of this book are for writing your songs. At the beginning of the "My Songs" section on page 11, there is a table of contents to record the page numbers and titles of your songs so they'll be easy to find. Each song is provided a two-page spread.

For each song spread, use the space at the top of the left page to fill in basic information, including the date, song title, and tempo/feel of your song. The rest of the left page is for transcribing lyrics, and is divided into sections for verses, chorus, and bridge.

The right page of the song spread is for writing music. At the top you will enter the verse-chorus-bridge structure of your song. In the middle section you will write your song's melody in the provided staffs, adding chords or tabs above the staffs if you wish. At the bottom of the page are fret diagrams to write guitar fingerings (if applicable) for chords used in your songs.

You'll find "The Inspiration Pages" on pages 7 to 10, comprised of questions and exercises to prompt songwriting ideas, as well as quotes from famous musicians for tips and inspiration. Use the pocket on the inside back cover to store all those random song ideas you get when away from this journal.

HOW TO GET STARTED WRITING SONGS

Make inspiration happen! Since songwriting is an active process, don't sit around waiting for the muse to strike. You are influenced by experiences in your life, so get out into the world to do and see new things. You can also use the exercises in "The Inspiration Pages" of this journal as a jumpstart when your creativity feels blocked.

A good song is one with which listeners can identify. As a songwriter you must be willing to write about those hidden places in yourself that are most honest and genuine in order to evoke feeling in your audience. Be candid, and do not attempt to write what you think people want to hear.

A songwriter is a storyteller. In order to develop this ability you must strengthen your own powers of observation, and draw insight from your imagination, surroundings, and such arts as cinema and literature. As a storyteller your writing should be rich with texture and detail.

In order to capture your audience's attention both melodically and lyrically, the opening lines of your song are the most important. Don't reveal everything at once, though; instead unveil your story throughout the song.

Familiarize yourself with the basics of songwriting. Make a song compelling with a hook—a memorable lyric or melodic phrase that captures the main idea of the song.

Organize components of your song idea into the verse-chorus-bridge form, where the verses convey the story or theme, the chorus repeats the main message, and the bridge—often introducing a change in key or rhythm—adds a dimension of complexity.

Approach the process in a playful and lighthearted way.

Have fun!

- Work on multiple songs at a time and don't delete old unfinished ideas; they may apply to a future song.
- Avoid clichés.
- Make writing appointments with yourself.
- Teach others to play and write. You will be surprised by what you learn during the process.
- Include a hook—the part of a song you find yourself singing in the shower.
- Use a loud/soft dynamic in both the instrumental and vocal arrangements.
- Include tempo variances in your song.
- Collaborate with other musicians on songwriting.
- Use a thesaurus and rhyming dictionary.

TIPS

The Inspiration PAGES

As soon as your mind knows that it's on and it's supposed to produce some lines, either it doesn't or it produces things that are very predictable. And that's why I say I'm not interested in writing something that I thought about. I'm interested in discovering where my mind wants to go, or what object it wants to pick up.

—Paul Simon

Go to a museum, find an interesting photograph or painting, and start writing lyrics based on what you see.

Each song has its own secret that's different from another song, and each has its own life. Sometimes it has to be teased out, whereas other times it might come fast. There are no laws about songwriting or producing.

—Mark Knopfler

Go to a busy place to write and observe people. Did you see a moment pass between two strangers? Write what you think their interaction was about; complete their narrative.

Who do you want to sing this song with?

How many instruments will be playing?

The idea of taking a song, envisioning the overall sound in my head, and then bringing the arrangement to life in the studio . . . well, that gives me satisfaction like nothing else. . . . No masterpiece ever came overnight. A person's masterpiece is something that you nurture along.

—Brian Wilson

Try playing in a different tuning.

I write the vocals last, because I wanted to invent the music first and push the music to the level that I had to compete against it.

—Axl Rose

Always keep a pad of paper with you for unexpected bursts of inspiration (near your bed, in the car, in your back pocket). Then you can tear out pages to store in the pocket at the back of this journal.

Pick the happiest, saddest, or funniest moment of your life and write about it for 10 minutes without stopping.

With songwriting I spend a lot of time living life, accruing all these experiences, journaling, and then by the time I get to the studio I'm teeming with the drive to write.

—Alanis Morissette

What social issues are most important to you? The arts are a reflection of what's happening in society, after all, so don't be shy about making a statement.

We must begin to make what I call "conscious choices," and to really recognize that we are the same. It's from that place in my heart that I write my songs.

—John Denver

Meditate for 15 minutes each day to help with focus and to tap into your subconscious mind.

Try to remember the details of your dreams.

> I wake up from dreams and go, "Wow, put this down on paper." The whole thing is strange. You hear the words, everything is right there in front of your face.
>
> —Michael Jackson

Drive or walk a different route than you usually do, or take public transportation and observe the people and places around you.

Watch live music and study the songs. Pay attention to the parts of songs that surprise you, as well as the ones that you can predict.

> It is only natural to pattern yourself after someone. If I wanted to be a painter, I might think about trying to be like van Gogh.... But you can't just copy somebody. If you like someone's work, the important thing is to be exposed to everything that person has been exposed to.
>
> —Bob Dylan

Role play. Put yourself in the place of the character in your song.

> I'm an untrained musician. Untrained musicians don't really have any music theory, they don't have a lot of rules. We break the rules, but it's mostly because we don't know what the rules are. It's easy for us to go to certain places, so I'm not surprised that a lot of people were amused by my songwriting style.
>
> —Frank Black

Just start playing and see what happens. What are you hearing in your head? Write down thoughts, melodies, things that are on your mind.

Open up a photo album. Visit family and friends.

My style of songwriting is influenced by cinema. I'm a frustrated filmmaker. A fan once said to me, "Girl, you make me see pictures in my head!" and I took that as a great compliment. That's exactly my intention.

—Joni Mitchell

Take a walk outside in nature. Did you see something beautiful or odd today? What did it make you feel?

What would you say to a former lover?

The best songwriting comes from being as creative as you can and editing it down to the good bits, essentially.

—Alex Kapranos

What is loss? What does longing feel like?

My songwriting is like extending a hand to the listener.

—Dave Grohl

MY SONGS

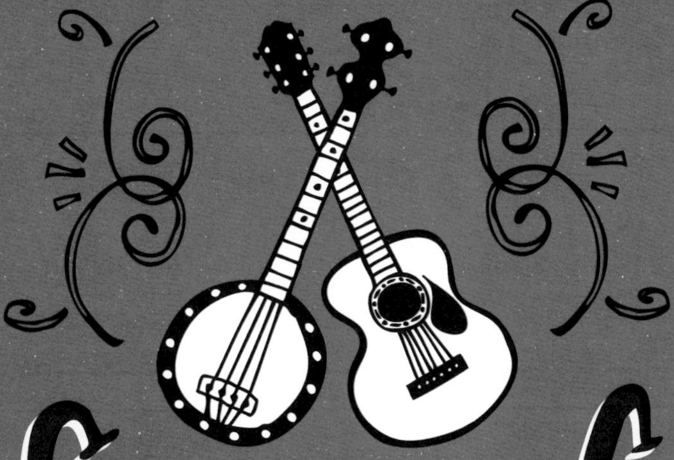

MY SONGS

TABLE of CONTENTS

SONG TITLE   PAGE

12

SONG TITLE   PAGE

SONG TITLE   PAGE

SONG TITLE: _____

_____

TEMPO/FEEL: _____

LYRICS

VERSE _____

CHORUS _____

BRIDGE _____

VERSE _____

VERSE _____

VERSE _____

16

MUSIC

Write song structure: VERSE=V, CHORUS=C, BRIDGE=B (V C V C B V C B)

- -

MELODY: write in melody and write chord names above staff lines.

ERSE

HORUS

RIDGE

HORDS:
Write guitar
ingerings used.

SONG TITLE: _____

_____

TEMPO/FEEL: _____

LYRICS

VERSE _____
_____
_____
_____

CHORUS _____
_____
_____
_____

BRIDGE _____
_____
_____
_____

VERSE _____
_____
_____
_____

VERSE _____
_____
_____
_____

VERSE _____
_____
_____

MUSIC

Write song structure: VERSE=V, CHORUS=C, BRIDGE=B (V C V C B V C B)

MELODY: write in melody and write chord names above staff lines.

VERSE

CHORUS

BRIDGE

CHORDS:
Write guitar
fingerings used.

SONG TITLE: _____

_____

TEMPO/FEEL: _____

LYRICS

VERSE _____
_____
_____
_____

CHORUS _____
_____
_____
_____

BRIDGE _____
_____
_____
_____

VERSE _____
_____
_____
_____

VERSE _____
_____
_____
_____

VERSE _____
_____
_____

MUSIC

Write song structure: VERSE=V, CHORUS=C, BRIDGE=B (V C V C B V C B)

MELODY: write in melody and write chord names above staff lines.

VERSE

CHORUS

BRIDGE

CHORDS:
Write guitar
fingerings used.

SONG TITLE: _____

_____

TEMPO/FEEL: _____

LYRICS

VERSE _____
_____
_____
_____

CHORUS _____
_____
_____
_____

BRIDGE _____
_____
_____
_____

VERSE _____
_____
_____
_____

VERSE _____
_____
_____
_____

VERSE _____
_____
_____
_____

MUSIC

Write song structure: VERSE=V, CHORUS=C, BRIDGE=B (V C V C B V C B)

MELODY: write in melody and write chord names above staff lines.

VERSE

CHORUS

BRIDGE

CHORDS:
Write guitar
fingerings used.

SONG TITLE: _____

_____

TEMPO/FEEL: _____

LYRICS

VERSE _____
_____
_____
_____

CHORUS _____
_____
_____
_____
_____

BRIDGE _____
_____
_____
_____
_____

VERSE _____
_____
_____
_____
_____

VERSE _____
_____
_____
_____

VERSE _____
_____
_____

MUSIC

Write song structure: VERSE=V, CHORUS=C, BRIDGE=B (V C V C B V C B)

- -

MELODY: write in melody and write chord names above staff lines.

VERSE

CHORUS

BRIDGE

CHORDS:
Write guitar
fingerings used.

SONG TITLE: _____

_____

TEMPO/FEEL: _____

LYRICS

VERSE _____
_____
_____
_____

CHORUS _____
_____
_____
_____

BRIDGE _____
_____
_____
_____

VERSE _____
_____
_____
_____

VERSE _____
_____
_____
_____

VERSE _____
_____
_____

MUSIC

Write song structure: VERSE=V, CHORUS=C, BRIDGE=B (V C V C B V C B)

MELODY: write in melody and write chord names above staff lines.

VERSE

CHORUS

BRIDGE

CHORDS:
Write guitar
fingerings used.

SONG TITLE: _____

_____

TEMPO/FEEL: _____

LYRICS

VERSE _____

CHORUS _____

BRIDGE _____

VERSE _____

VERSE _____

VERSE _____

28

MUSIC

Write song structure: VERSE=V, CHORUS=C, BRIDGE=B (V C V C B V C B)

MELODY: write in melody and write chord names above staff lines.

VERSE

CHORUS

BRIDGE

CHORDS:
Write guitar
fingerings used.

date

SONG TITLE: _____

_____

TEMPO/FEEL: _____

LYRICS

VERSE _____

_____

_____

_____

CHORUS _____

_____

_____

_____

BRIDGE _____

_____

_____

_____

VERSE _____

_____

_____

_____

VERSE _____

_____

_____

_____

VERSE _____

_____

MUSIC

Write song structure: VERSE=V, CHORUS=C, BRIDGE=B (V C V C B V C B)

MELODY: write in melody and write chord names above staff lines.

VERSE

CHORUS

BRIDGE

CHORDS:
Write guitar
fingerings used.

SONG TITLE: _____
_____

TEMPO/FEEL: _____

LYRICS

VERSE _____
_____
_____
_____

CHORUS _____
_____
_____
_____

BRIDGE _____
_____
_____
_____

VERSE _____
_____
_____
_____

VERSE _____
_____
_____
_____

VERSE _____
_____
_____

MUSIC

Write song structure: VERSE=V, CHORUS=C, BRIDGE=B (V C V C B V C B)

MELODY: write in melody and write chord names above staff lines.

VERSE

CHORUS

BRIDGE

CHORDS:
Write guitar
fingerings used.

SONG TITLE: _____
_____

TEMPO/FEEL: _____

LYRICS

VERSE _____
_____
_____
_____

CHORUS _____
_____
_____
_____

BRIDGE _____
_____
_____
_____

VERSE _____
_____
_____
_____

VERSE _____
_____
_____
_____

VERSE _____
_____
_____

MUSIC

Write song structure: VERSE=V, CHORUS=C, BRIDGE=B (V C V C B V C B)

MELODY: write in melody and write chord names above staff lines.

VERSE

CHORUS

BRIDGE

CHORDS:
Write guitar
fingerings used.

35

SONG TITLE: _____

_____

TEMPO/FEEL: _____

LYRICS

VERSE _____
_____
_____
_____

CHORUS _____
_____
_____
_____

BRIDGE _____
_____
_____
_____

VERSE _____
_____
_____
_____

VERSE _____
_____
_____
_____

VERSE _____
_____
_____

MUSIC

Write song structure: VERSE=V, CHORUS=C, BRIDGE=B (V C V C B V C B)

- -

MELODY: write in melody and write chord names above staff lines.

VERSE

CHORUS

BRIDGE

CHORDS:
Write guitar
fingerings used.

SONG TITLE: _____

_____

TEMPO/FEEL: _____

LYRICS

VERSE _____
_____
_____
_____
_____

CHORUS _____
_____
_____
_____
_____

BRIDGE _____
_____
_____
_____
_____

VERSE _____
_____
_____
_____

VERSE _____
_____
_____
_____

VERSE _____
_____
_____

MUSIC

Write song structure: VERSE=V, CHORUS=C, BRIDGE=B (V C V C B V C B)

- -

MELODY: write in melody and write chord names above staff lines.

VERSE

CHORUS

BRIDGE

CHORDS:
Write guitar
fingerings used.

SONG TITLE: _____

_____

TEMPO/FEEL: _____

LYRICS

VERSE _____
_____
_____
_____

CHORUS _____
_____
_____
_____

BRIDGE _____
_____
_____
_____

VERSE _____
_____
_____
_____

VERSE _____
_____
_____
_____

VERSE _____
_____

MUSIC

Write song structure: VERSE=V, CHORUS=C, BRIDGE=B (V C V C B V C B)

MELODY: write in melody and write chord names above staff lines.

VERSE

CHORUS

BRIDGE

CHORDS:
Write guitar
fingerings used.

SONG TITLE: _____

_____

TEMPO/FEEL: _____

LYRICS

VERSE _____
_____
_____
_____
_____

CHORUS _____
_____
_____
_____
_____

BRIDGE _____
_____
_____
_____
_____

VERSE _____
_____
_____
_____
_____

VERSE _____
_____
_____
_____
_____

VERSE _____
_____

MUSIC

Write song structure: VERSE=V, CHORUS=C, BRIDGE=B (V C V C B V C B)

- -

MELODY: write in melody and write chord names above staff lines.

VERSE

CHORUS

BRIDGE

CHORDS:
Write guitar
fingerings used.

SONG TITLE: _____

_____

TEMPO/FEEL: _____

LYRICS

VERSE _____
_____
_____
_____

CHORUS _____
_____
_____
_____

BRIDGE _____
_____
_____
_____

VERSE _____
_____
_____
_____

VERSE _____
_____
_____
_____

VERSE _____
_____
_____

MUSIC

Write song structure: VERSE=V, CHORUS=C, BRIDGE=B (V C V C B V C B)

MELODY: write in melody and write chord names above staff lines.

VERSE

CHORUS

BRIDGE

CHORDS:
Write guitar
fingerings used.

SONG TITLE: _____

_____

TEMPO/FEEL: _____

LYRICS

VERSE _____
_____
_____
_____

CHORUS _____
_____
_____
_____

BRIDGE _____
_____
_____
_____

VERSE _____
_____
_____
_____

VERSE _____
_____
_____
_____

VERSE _____
_____
_____

MUSIC

Write song structure: VERSE=V, CHORUS=C, BRIDGE=B (V C V C B V C B)

MELODY: write in melody and write chord names above staff lines.

VERSE

CHORUS

BRIDGE

CHORDS:
Write guitar
fingerings used.

SONG TITLE: _____
_____

TEMPO/FEEL: _____

LYRICS

VERSE _____
_____
_____
_____

CHORUS _____
_____
_____
_____

BRIDGE _____
_____
_____
_____

VERSE _____
_____
_____
_____

VERSE _____
_____
_____
_____

VERSE _____
_____
_____

MUSIC

Write song structure: VERSE=V, CHORUS=C, BRIDGE=B (V C V C B V C B)

- -

MELODY: write in melody and write chord names above staff lines.

VERSE

CHORUS

BRIDGE

CHORDS:
Write guitar
fingerings used.

date

SONG TITLE: _____

_____

TEMPO/FEEL: _____

LYRICS

VERSE _____
_____
_____
_____

CHORUS _____
_____
_____
_____
_____

BRIDGE _____
_____
_____
_____

VERSE _____
_____
_____
_____

VERSE _____
_____
_____
_____

VERSE _____
_____
_____

MUSIC

Write song structure: VERSE=V, CHORUS=C, BRIDGE=B (V C V C B V C B)

MELODY: write in melody and write chord names above staff lines.

VERSE

CHORUS

BRIDGE

CHORDS:
Write guitar
fingerings used.

SONG TITLE: _____

_____

TEMPO/FEEL: _____

LYRICS

VERSE _____

_____

_____

_____

CHORUS _____

_____

_____

_____

BRIDGE _____

_____

_____

_____

VERSE _____

_____

_____

_____

VERSE _____

_____

_____

_____

VERSE _____

_____

_____

MUSIC

Write song structure: VERSE=V, CHORUS=C, BRIDGE=B (V C V C B V C B)

MELODY: write in melody and write chord names above staff lines.

ERSE

HORUS

RIDGE

HORDS:
Write guitar
ingerings used.

SONG TITLE: _____

_____

TEMPO/FEEL: _____

LYRICS

VERSE _____

_____

_____

_____

CHORUS _____

_____

_____

_____

BRIDGE _____

_____

_____

_____

VERSE _____

_____

_____

_____

VERSE _____

_____

_____

_____

VERSE _____

_____

_____

MUSIC

Write song structure: VERSE=V, CHORUS=C, BRIDGE=B (V C V C B V C B)

- -

MELODY: write in melody and write chord names above staff lines.

VERSE

CHORUS

BRIDGE

CHORDS:
Write guitar
fingerings used.

SONG TITLE: _____

_____

TEMPO/FEEL: _____

LYRICS

VERSE _____

_____

_____

_____

CHORUS _____

_____

_____

_____

_____

BRIDGE _____

_____

_____

_____

_____

VERSE _____

_____

_____

_____

_____

VERSE _____

_____

_____

_____

_____

VERSE _____

_____

_____

MUSIC

Write song structure: VERSE=V, CHORUS=C, BRIDGE=B (V C V C B V C B)

- -

MELODY: write in melody and write chord names above staff lines.

VERSE

CHORUS

BRIDGE

CHORDS:
Write guitar
fingerings used.

SONG TITLE: _____

_____

TEMPO/FEEL: _____

LYRICS

VERSE _____
_____
_____
_____

CHORUS _____
_____
_____
_____

BRIDGE _____
_____
_____
_____

VERSE _____
_____
_____
_____

VERSE _____
_____
_____
_____

VERSE _____
_____

MUSIC

Write song structure: VERSE=V, CHORUS=C, BRIDGE=B (V C V C B V C B)

- -

MELODY: write in melody and write chord names above staff lines.

VERSE

CHORUS

BRIDGE

CHORDS:
Write guitar
fingerings used.

SONG TITLE: _____

_____

TEMPO/FEEL: _____

LYRICS

VERSE _____
_____
_____
_____

CHORUS _____
_____
_____
_____

BRIDGE _____
_____
_____
_____

VERSE _____
_____
_____
_____

VERSE _____
_____
_____
_____

VERSE _____
_____
_____

MUSIC

Write song structure: VERSE=V, CHORUS=C, BRIDGE=B (V C V C B V C B)

- -

MELODY: write in melody and write chord names above staff lines.

VERSE

CHORUS

BRIDGE

CHORDS:
Write guitar
fingerings used.

SONG TITLE: _____

_____

TEMPO/FEEL: _____

LYRICS

VERSE _____
_____
_____
_____

CHORUS _____
_____
_____
_____

BRIDGE _____
_____
_____
_____

VERSE _____
_____
_____
_____

VERSE _____
_____
_____
_____

VERSE _____
_____

MUSIC

Write song structure: VERSE=V, CHORUS=C, BRIDGE=B (V C V C B V C B)

MELODY: write in melody and write chord names above staff lines.

VERSE

CHORUS

BRIDGE

CHORDS:
Write guitar
fingerings used.

SONG TITLE: _____

_____

TEMPO/FEEL: _____

LYRICS

VERSE _____
_____
_____
_____

CHORUS _____
_____
_____
_____
_____

BRIDGE _____
_____
_____
_____

VERSE _____
_____
_____
_____

VERSE _____
_____
_____
_____

VERSE _____
_____
_____

MUSIC

Write song structure: VERSE=V, CHORUS=C, BRIDGE=B (V C V C B V C B)

- -

MELODY: write in melody and write chord names above staff lines.

VERSE

CHORUS

BRIDGE

CHORDS:
Write guitar
fingerings used.

SONG TITLE: _____

_____

TEMPO/FEEL: _____

LYRICS

VERSE _____
_____
_____
_____

CHORUS _____
_____
_____
_____

BRIDGE _____
_____
_____
_____

VERSE _____
_____
_____
_____

VERSE _____
_____
_____
_____

VERSE _____
_____
_____

MUSIC

Write song structure: VERSE=V, CHORUS=C, BRIDGE=B (V C V C B V C B)

- -

MELODY: write in melody and write chord names above staff lines.

VERSE

CHORUS

BRIDGE

CHORDS:
Write guitar
fingerings used.

SONG TITLE: _____

_____

TEMPO/FEEL: _____

LYRICS

VERSE _____

_____

_____

_____

_____

CHORUS _____

_____

_____

_____

BRIDGE _____

_____

_____

_____

_____

VERSE _____

_____

_____

_____

VERSE _____

_____

_____

_____

VERSE _____

_____

MUSIC

Write song structure: VERSE=V, CHORUS=C, BRIDGE=B (V C V C B V C B)

- -

MELODY: write in melody and write chord names above staff lines.

VERSE

CHORUS

BRIDGE

CHORDS:
Write guitar
fingerings used.

SONG TITLE: _____

_____

TEMPO/FEEL: _____

LYRICS

VERSE _____
_____
_____
_____

CHORUS _____
_____
_____
_____

BRIDGE _____
_____
_____
_____

VERSE _____
_____
_____
_____

VERSE _____
_____
_____
_____

VERSE _____
_____

MUSIC

Write song structure: VERSE=V, CHORUS=C, BRIDGE=B (V C V C B V C B)

- -

MELODY: write in melody and write chord names above staff lines.

VERSE

CHORUS

BRIDGE

CHORDS:
Write guitar
fingerings used.

SONG TITLE: _____

_____

TEMPO/FEEL: _____

LYRICS

VERSE _____

_____

_____

_____

CHORUS _____

_____

_____

_____

BRIDGE _____

_____

_____

_____

VERSE _____

_____

_____

_____

VERSE _____

_____

_____

_____

VERSE _____

_____

_____

MUSIC

Write song structure: VERSE=V, CHORUS=C, BRIDGE=B (V C V C B V C B)

MELODY: write in melody and write chord names above staff lines.

ERSE

HORUS

RIDGE

HORDS:
Write guitar
ingerings used.

73

date

SONG TITLE: _____

_____

TEMPO/FEEL: _____

LYRICS

VERSE _____
_____
_____
_____

CHORUS _____
_____
_____
_____

BRIDGE _____
_____
_____
_____

VERSE _____
_____
_____
_____

VERSE _____
_____
_____
_____

VERSE _____
_____
_____

74

MUSIC

Write song structure: VERSE=V, CHORUS=C, BRIDGE=B (V C V C B V C B)

- -

MELODY: write in melody and write chord names above staff lines.

VERSE

CHORUS

BRIDGE

CHORDS:
Write guitar
fingerings used.

SONG TITLE: _____

_____

TEMPO/FEEL: _____

LYRICS

VERSE _____
_____
_____
_____

CHORUS _____
_____
_____
_____

BRIDGE _____
_____
_____
_____

VERSE _____
_____
_____
_____

VERSE _____
_____
_____
_____

VERSE _____
_____

MUSIC

Write song structure: VERSE=V, CHORUS=C, BRIDGE=B (V C V C B V C B)

- -

MELODY: write in melody and write chord names above staff lines.

VERSE

CHORUS

BRIDGE

CHORDS:
Write guitar
fingerings used.

SONG TITLE: _____
_____

TEMPO/FEEL: _____

LYRICS

VERSE _____
_____
_____
_____

CHORUS _____
_____
_____
_____

BRIDGE _____
_____
_____
_____

VERSE _____
_____
_____
_____

VERSE _____
_____
_____
_____

VERSE _____
_____
_____

MUSIC

Write song structure: VERSE=V, CHORUS=C, BRIDGE=B (V C V C B V C B)

- -

MELODY: write in melody and write chord names above staff lines.

VERSE

CHORUS

BRIDGE

CHORDS:
Write guitar
fingerings used.

SONG TITLE: _____

_____

TEMPO/FEEL: _____

LYRICS

VERSE _____

_____

_____

_____

CHORUS _____

_____

_____

_____

_____

BRIDGE _____

_____

_____

_____

_____

VERSE _____

_____

_____

_____

_____

VERSE _____

_____

_____

_____

VERSE _____

_____

_____

MUSIC

Write song structure: VERSE=V, CHORUS=C, BRIDGE=B (V C V C B V C B)

MELODY: write in melody and write chord names above staff lines.

VERSE

CHORUS

BRIDGE

CHORDS:
Write guitar
fingerings used.

SONG TITLE: _____

_____

TEMPO/FEEL: _____

LYRICS

VERSE _____

_____

_____

_____

CHORUS _____

_____

_____

_____

BRIDGE _____

_____

_____

_____

VERSE _____

_____

_____

_____

VERSE _____

_____

_____

_____

VERSE _____

_____

_____

MUSIC

Write song structure: VERSE=V, CHORUS=C, BRIDGE=B (V C V C B V C B)

MELODY: write in melody and write chord names above staff lines.

VERSE

CHORUS

BRIDGE

CHORDS:
Write guitar
fingerings used.

SONG TITLE: _____

_____

TEMPO/FEEL: _____

LYRICS

VERSE _____

_____

_____

_____

CHORUS _____

_____

_____

_____

BRIDGE _____

_____

_____

_____

VERSE _____

_____

_____

_____

VERSE _____

_____

_____

_____

VERSE _____

_____

_____

MUSIC

Write song structure: VERSE=V, CHORUS=C, BRIDGE=B (V C V C B V C B)

- -

MELODY: write in melody and write chord names above staff lines.

VERSE

CHORUS

BRIDGE

CHORDS:
Write guitar
fingerings used.

SONG TITLE: _____
_____

TEMPO/FEEL: _____

LYRICS

VERSE _____
_____
_____
_____

CHORUS _____
_____
_____
_____
_____

BRIDGE _____
_____
_____
_____

VERSE _____
_____
_____
_____

VERSE _____
_____
_____
_____

VERSE _____
_____
_____

MUSIC

Write song structure: VERSE=V, CHORUS=C, BRIDGE=B (V C V C B V C B)

MELODY: write in melody and write chord names above staff lines.

VERSE

CHORUS

BRIDGE

CHORDS:
Write guitar
fingerings used.

SONG TITLE: _____

_____

TEMPO/FEEL: _____

LYRICS

VERSE _____

_____

_____

_____

CHORUS _____

_____

_____

_____

BRIDGE _____

_____

_____

_____

VERSE _____

_____

_____

_____

VERSE _____

_____

_____

_____

VERSE _____

_____

MUSIC

Write song structure: VERSE=V, CHORUS=C, BRIDGE=B (V C V C B V C B)

MELODY: write in melody and write chord names above staff lines.

VERSE

CHORUS

BRIDGE

CHORDS:
Write guitar
fingerings used.

SONG TITLE: _____

_____

TEMPO/FEEL: _____

LYRICS

VERSE _____
_____
_____
_____

CHORUS _____
_____
_____
_____

BRIDGE _____
_____
_____
_____

VERSE _____
_____
_____
_____

VERSE _____
_____
_____
_____

VERSE _____
_____
_____

MUSIC

Write song structure: VERSE=V, CHORUS=C, BRIDGE=B (V C V C B V C B)

MELODY: write in melody and write chord names above staff lines.

VERSE

CHORUS

BRIDGE

CHORDS:
Write guitar
fingerings used.

SONG TITLE: _____

_____

TEMPO/FEEL: _____

LYRICS

VERSE _____
_____
_____
_____

CHORUS _____
_____
_____
_____

BRIDGE _____
_____
_____
_____

VERSE _____
_____
_____
_____

VERSE _____
_____
_____
_____

VERSE _____
_____
_____

MUSIC

Write song structure: VERSE=V, CHORUS=C, BRIDGE=B (V C V C B V C B)

MELODY: write in melody and write chord names above staff lines.

VERSE

CHORUS

BRIDGE

CHORDS:
Write guitar
fingerings used.

SONG TITLE: _____

_____

TEMPO/FEEL: _____

LYRICS

VERSE _____
_____
_____
_____

CHORUS _____
_____
_____
_____

BRIDGE _____
_____
_____
_____

VERSE _____
_____
_____
_____

VERSE _____
_____
_____
_____

VERSE _____
_____
_____

MUSIC

Write song structure: VERSE=V, CHORUS=C, BRIDGE=B (V C V C B V C B)

MELODY: write in melody and write chord names above staff lines.

VERSE

CHORUS

BRIDGE

CHORDS:
Write guitar
fingerings used.

SONG TITLE: _____

_____

TEMPO/FEEL: _____

LYRICS

VERSE _____

_____

_____

_____

CHORUS _____

_____

_____

_____

BRIDGE _____

_____

_____

_____

VERSE _____

_____

_____

_____

VERSE _____

_____

_____

_____

VERSE _____

_____

_____

MUSIC

Write song structure: VERSE=V, CHORUS=C, BRIDGE=B (V C V C B V C B)

- -

MELODY: write in melody and write chord names above staff lines.

VERSE

CHORUS

BRIDGE

CHORDS:
Write guitar
fingerings used.

SONG TITLE: _____

_____

TEMPO/FEEL: _____

LYRICS

VERSE _____

_____
_____
_____
_____

CHORUS _____

_____
_____
_____
_____

BRIDGE _____

_____
_____
_____
_____

VERSE _____

_____
_____
_____
_____

VERSE _____

_____
_____
_____
_____

VERSE _____

_____
_____

MUSIC

Write song structure: VERSE=V, CHORUS=C, BRIDGE=B (V C V C B V C B)

- -

MELODY: write in melody and write chord names above staff lines.

VERSE

CHORUS

BRIDGE

CHORDS:
Write guitar
fingerings used.

SONG TITLE: _____
_____

TEMPO/FEEL: _____

LYRICS

VERSE _____
_____
_____
_____

CHORUS _____
_____
_____
_____

BRIDGE _____
_____
_____
_____

VERSE _____
_____
_____
_____

VERSE _____
_____
_____
_____

VERSE _____
_____
_____

MUSIC

Write song structure: VERSE=V, CHORUS=C, BRIDGE=B (V C V C B V C B)

MELODY: write in melody and write chord names above staff lines.

VERSE

CHORUS

BRIDGE

CHORDS:
Write guitar
fingerings used.

SONG TITLE: _____

_____

TEMPO/FEEL: _____

LYRICS

VERSE _____
_____
_____
_____

CHORUS _____
_____
_____
_____

BRIDGE _____
_____
_____
_____

VERSE _____
_____
_____
_____

VERSE _____
_____
_____
_____

VERSE _____
_____
_____

MUSIC

Write song structure: VERSE=V, CHORUS=C, BRIDGE=B (V C V C B V C B)

MELODY: write in melody and write chord names above staff lines.

VERSE

CHORUS

BRIDGE

CHORDS:
Write guitar
fingerings used.

SONG TITLE: _____

_____

TEMPO/FEEL: _____

LYRICS

VERSE _____

_____

_____

_____

CHORUS _____

_____

_____

_____

BRIDGE _____

_____

_____

_____

VERSE _____

_____

_____

_____

VERSE _____

_____

_____

_____

VERSE _____

_____

_____

MUSIC

Write song structure: VERSE=V, CHORUS=C, BRIDGE=B (V C V C B V C B)

MELODY: write in melody and write chord names above staff lines.

VERSE

CHORUS

BRIDGE

CHORDS:
Write guitar
fingerings used.

SONG TITLE: _____

_____

TEMPO/FEEL: _____

LYRICS

VERSE _____
_____
_____
_____

CHORUS _____
_____
_____
_____

BRIDGE _____
_____
_____
_____

VERSE _____
_____
_____
_____

VERSE _____
_____
_____

VERSE _____
_____
_____

MUSIC

Write song structure: VERSE=V, CHORUS=C, BRIDGE=B (V C V C B V C B)

MELODY: write in melody and write chord names above staff lines.

VERSE

CHORUS

BRIDGE

CHORDS:
Write guitar
fingerings used.

SONG TITLE: _____

_____

TEMPO/FEEL: _____

LYRICS

VERSE _____
_____
_____
_____

CHORUS _____
_____
_____
_____

BRIDGE _____
_____
_____
_____

VERSE _____
_____
_____
_____

VERSE _____
_____
_____
_____

VERSE _____
_____

MUSIC

Write song structure: VERSE=V, CHORUS=C, BRIDGE=B (V C V C B V C B)

- -

MELODY: write in melody and write chord names above staff lines.

VERSE

CHORUS

BRIDGE

CHORDS:
Write guitar
fingerings used.

SONG TITLE: _____

_____

TEMPO/FEEL: _____

LYRICS

VERSE _____
_____
_____
_____

CHORUS _____
_____
_____
_____

BRIDGE _____
_____
_____
_____

VERSE _____
_____
_____
_____

VERSE _____
_____
_____
_____

VERSE _____
_____
_____

MUSIC

Write song structure: VERSE=V, CHORUS=C, BRIDGE=B (V C V C B V C B)

MELODY: write in melody and write chord names above staff lines.

VERSE

CHORUS

BRIDGE

CHORDS:
Write guitar
fingerings used.

SONG TITLE: _____

_____

TEMPO/FEEL: _____

LYRICS

VERSE _____

_____

_____

_____

CHORUS _____

_____

_____

_____

BRIDGE _____

_____

_____

_____

VERSE _____

_____

_____

_____

VERSE _____

_____

_____

_____

VERSE _____

_____

_____

MUSIC

Write song structure: VERSE=V, CHORUS=C, BRIDGE=B (V C V C B V C B)

- -

MELODY: write in melody and write chord names above staff lines.

VERSE

CHORUS

BRIDGE

CHORDS:
Write guitar
fingerings used.

SONG TITLE: _____

_____

TEMPO/FEEL: _____

LYRICS

VERSE _____
_____
_____
_____
_____

CHORUS _____
_____
_____
_____
_____

BRIDGE _____
_____
_____
_____
_____

VERSE _____
_____
_____
_____
_____

VERSE _____
_____
_____
_____
_____

VERSE _____
_____
_____

114

MUSIC

Write song structure: VERSE=V, CHORUS=C, BRIDGE=B (V C V C B V C B)

MELODY: write in melody and write chord names above staff lines.

VERSE

CHORUS

BRIDGE

CHORDS:
Write guitar
fingerings used.

SONG TITLE: _____

_____

TEMPO/FEEL: _____

LYRICS

VERSE _____
_____
_____
_____

CHORUS _____
_____
_____
_____

BRIDGE _____
_____
_____
_____

VERSE _____
_____
_____
_____

VERSE _____
_____
_____
_____

VERSE _____
_____
_____

MUSIC

Write song structure: VERSE=V, CHORUS=C, BRIDGE=B (V C V C B V C B)

MELODY: write in melody and write chord names above staff lines.

VERSE

CHORUS

BRIDGE

CHORDS:
Write guitar
fingerings used.

117

SONG TITLE: _____
_____

TEMPO/FEEL: _____

LYRICS

VERSE _____
_____
_____
_____

CHORUS _____
_____
_____
_____

BRIDGE _____
_____
_____
_____

VERSE _____
_____
_____
_____

VERSE _____
_____
_____
_____

VERSE _____
_____
_____

MUSIC

Write song structure: VERSE=V, CHORUS=C, BRIDGE=B (V C V C B V C B)

MELODY: write in melody and write chord names above staff lines.

VERSE

CHORUS

BRIDGE

CHORDS:
Write guitar
fingerings used.

date

SONG TITLE: _____

_____

TEMPO/FEEL: _____

LYRICS

VERSE _____
_____
_____
_____

CHORUS _____
_____
_____
_____

BRIDGE _____
_____
_____
_____

VERSE _____
_____
_____
_____

VERSE _____
_____
_____
_____

VERSE _____
_____
_____

MUSIC

Write song structure: VERSE=V, CHORUS=C, BRIDGE=B (V C V C B V C B)

MELODY: write in melody and write chord names above staff lines.

VERSE

CHORUS

BRIDGE

CHORDS:
Write guitar
fingerings used.

SONG TITLE: _____

_____

TEMPO/FEEL: _____

LYRICS

VERSE _____

_____

_____

_____

CHORUS _____

_____

_____

_____

BRIDGE _____

_____

_____

_____

VERSE _____

_____

_____

_____

VERSE _____

_____

_____

_____

VERSE _____

_____

_____

MUSIC

Write song structure: VERSE=V, CHORUS=C, BRIDGE=B (V C V C B V C B)

MELODY: write in melody and write chord names above staff lines.

VERSE

CHORUS

BRIDGE

CHORDS:
Write guitar
fingerings used.

SONG TITLE: _____
_____

TEMPO/FEEL: _____

LYRICS

VERSE _____
_____
_____
_____

CHORUS _____
_____
_____
_____
_____

BRIDGE _____
_____
_____
_____

VERSE _____
_____
_____
_____

VERSE _____
_____
_____
_____

VERSE _____
_____
_____

MUSIC

Write song structure: VERSE=V, CHORUS=C, BRIDGE=B (V C V C B V C B)

MELODY: write in melody and write chord names above staff lines.

VERSE

CHORUS

BRIDGE

CHORDS:
Write guitar
fingerings used.

SONG TITLE: _____

_____

TEMPO/FEEL: _____

LYRICS

VERSE _____

_____

_____

_____

CHORUS _____

_____

_____

_____

_____

BRIDGE _____

_____

_____

_____

VERSE _____

_____

_____

_____

_____

VERSE _____

_____

_____

_____

VERSE _____

_____

_____

MUSIC

Write song structure: VERSE=V, CHORUS=C, BRIDGE=B (V C V C B V C B)

- -

MELODY: write in melody and write chord names above staff lines.

VERSE

CHORUS

BRIDGE

CHORDS:
Write guitar
fingerings used.

SONG TITLE: _____

_____

TEMPO/FEEL: _____

LYRICS

VERSE _____

_____

_____

_____

CHORUS _____

_____

_____

_____

BRIDGE _____

_____

_____

_____

VERSE _____

_____

_____

_____

VERSE _____

_____

_____

_____

VERSE _____

_____

_____

MUSIC

Write song structure: VERSE=V, CHORUS=C, BRIDGE=B (V C V C B V C B)

- -

MELODY: write in melody and write chord names above staff lines.

VERSE

CHORUS

BRIDGE

CHORDS:
Write guitar
fingerings used.

SONG TITLE: _____
_____

TEMPO/FEEL: _____

LYRICS

VERSE _____
_____
_____
_____
_____

CHORUS _____
_____
_____
_____
_____

BRIDGE _____
_____
_____
_____
_____

VERSE _____
_____
_____
_____
_____

VERSE _____
_____
_____
_____
_____

VERSE _____
_____
_____

MUSIC

Write song structure: VERSE=V, CHORUS=C, BRIDGE=B (V C V C B V C B)

MELODY: write in melody and write chord names above staff lines.

VERSE

CHORUS

BRIDGE

CHORDS:
Write guitar
fingerings used.

SONG TITLE: _____

_____

TEMPO/FEEL: _____

LYRICS

VERSE _____
_____
_____
_____
_____

CHORUS _____
_____
_____
_____
_____

BRIDGE _____
_____
_____
_____
_____

VERSE _____
_____
_____
_____
_____

VERSE _____
_____
_____
_____
_____

VERSE _____
_____
_____

MUSIC

Write song structure: VERSE=V, CHORUS=C, BRIDGE=B (V C V C B V C B)

MELODY: write in melody and write chord names above staff lines.

VERSE

CHORUS

BRIDGE

CHORDS:
Write guitar
fingerings used.

SONG TITLE: _____

_____

TEMPO/FEEL: _____

LYRICS

VERSE _____
_____
_____
_____
_____

CHORUS _____
_____
_____
_____
_____

BRIDGE _____
_____
_____
_____
_____

VERSE _____
_____
_____
_____
_____

VERSE _____
_____
_____
_____

VERSE _____
_____
_____

MUSIC

Write song structure: VERSE=V, CHORUS=C, BRIDGE=B (V C V C B V C B)

MELODY: write in melody and write chord names above staff lines.

VERSE

CHORUS

BRIDGE

CHORDS:
Write guitar
fingerings used.

SONG TITLE: _____

_____

TEMPO/FEEL: _____

LYRICS

VERSE _____
_____
_____
_____

CHORUS _____
_____
_____
_____

BRIDGE _____
_____
_____
_____

VERSE _____
_____
_____
_____

VERSE _____
_____
_____
_____

VERSE _____
_____
_____

MUSIC

Write song structure: VERSE=V, CHORUS=C, BRIDGE=B (V C V C B V C B)

- -

MELODY: write in melody and write chord names above staff lines.

VERSE

CHORUS

BRIDGE

CHORDS:
Write guitar
fingerings used.

137

date

SONG TITLE: _____

_____

TEMPO/FEEL: _____

LYRICS

VERSE _____

_____

_____

_____

CHORUS _____

_____

_____

_____

_____

BRIDGE _____

_____

_____

_____

VERSE _____

_____

_____

_____

VERSE _____

_____

_____

_____

VERSE _____

_____

_____

(138) _____

MUSIC

Write song structure: VERSE=V, CHORUS=C, BRIDGE=B (V C V C B V C B)

MELODY: write in melody and write chord names above staff lines.

VERSE

CHORUS

BRIDGE

CHORDS:
Write guitar
fingerings used.

SONG TITLE: _____

_____

TEMPO/FEEL: _____

LYRICS

VERSE _____

_____

_____

_____

CHORUS _____

_____

_____

_____

BRIDGE _____

_____

_____

_____

VERSE _____

_____

_____

_____

VERSE _____

_____

_____

_____

VERSE _____

_____

MUSIC

Write song structure: VERSE=V, CHORUS=C, BRIDGE=B (V C V C B V C B)

MELODY: write in melody and write chord names above staff lines.

VERSE

CHORUS

BRIDGE

CHORDS:
Write guitar
fingerings used.

SONG TITLE: _____

_____

TEMPO/FEEL: _____

LYRICS

VERSE _____

CHORUS _____

BRIDGE _____

VERSE _____

VERSE _____

VERSE _____

MUSIC

Write song structure: VERSE=V, CHORUS=C, BRIDGE=B (V C V C B V C B)

MELODY: write in melody and write chord names above staff lines.

VERSE

CHORUS

BRIDGE

CHORDS:
Write guitar
fingerings used.

SONG TITLE: _____

_____

TEMPO/FEEL: _____

LYRICS

VERSE _____

_____

_____

_____

CHORUS _____

_____

_____

_____

BRIDGE _____

_____

_____

_____

VERSE _____

_____

_____

_____

VERSE _____

_____

_____

_____

VERSE _____

_____

_____

MUSIC

Write song structure: VERSE=V, CHORUS=C, BRIDGE=B (V C V C B V C B)

MELODY: write in melody and write chord names above staff lines.

VERSE

CHORUS

BRIDGE

CHORDS:
Write guitar
fingerings used.

date

SONG TITLE: _____

_____

TEMPO/FEEL: _____

LYRICS

VERSE _____
_____
_____
_____

CHORUS _____
_____
_____
_____

BRIDGE _____
_____
_____
_____

VERSE _____
_____
_____
_____

VERSE _____
_____
_____
_____

VERSE _____
_____
_____

146

MUSIC

Write song structure: VERSE=V, CHORUS=C, BRIDGE=B (V C V C B V C B)

- -

MELODY: write in melody and write chord names above staff lines.

VERSE

CHORUS

BRIDGE

CHORDS:
Write guitar
fingerings used.

SONG TITLE: _____

_____

TEMPO/FEEL: _____

LYRICS

VERSE _____

_____

_____

_____

CHORUS _____

_____

_____

_____

BRIDGE _____

_____

_____

_____

VERSE _____

_____

_____

_____

VERSE _____

_____

_____

_____

VERSE _____

_____

_____

MUSIC

Write song structure: VERSE=V, CHORUS=C, BRIDGE=B (V C V C B V C B)

MELODY: write in melody and write chord names above staff lines.

VERSE

CHORUS

BRIDGE

CHORDS:
Write guitar
fingerings used.

SONG TITLE: _____

_____

TEMPO/FEEL: _____

LYRICS

VERSE _____

_____

_____

_____

CHORUS _____

_____

_____

_____

BRIDGE _____

_____

_____

_____

VERSE _____

_____

_____

_____

VERSE _____

_____

_____

_____

VERSE _____

_____

_____

(150) _____

MUSIC

Write song structure: VERSE=V, CHORUS=C, BRIDGE=B (V C V C B V C B)

MELODY: write in melody and write chord names above staff lines.

VERSE

CHORUS

BRIDGE

CHORDS:
Write guitar
fingerings used.

SONG TITLE: _____

_____

TEMPO/FEEL: _____

LYRICS

VERSE _____

_____

_____

_____

CHORUS _____

_____

_____

_____

BRIDGE _____

_____

_____

_____

VERSE _____

_____

_____

_____

VERSE _____

_____

_____

_____

VERSE _____

_____

MUSIC

Write song structure: VERSE=V, CHORUS=C, BRIDGE=B (V C V C B V C B)

- -

MELODY: write in melody and write chord names above staff lines.

VERSE

CHORUS

BRIDGE

CHORDS:
Write guitar
fingerings used.

SONG TITLE: _____

_____

TEMPO/FEEL: _____

LYRICS

VERSE _____
_____
_____
_____

CHORUS _____
_____
_____
_____

BRIDGE _____
_____
_____
_____

VERSE _____
_____
_____
_____

VERSE _____
_____
_____

VERSE _____
_____
_____

MUSIC

Write song structure: VERSE=V, CHORUS=C, BRIDGE=B (V C V C B V C B)

- -

MELODY: write in melody and write chord names above staff lines.

VERSE

CHORUS

BRIDGE

CHORDS:
Write guitar
fingerings used.

date

SONG TITLE: _____

_____

TEMPO/FEEL: _____

LYRICS

VERSE _____
_____
_____
_____

CHORUS _____
_____
_____
_____

BRIDGE _____
_____
_____
_____

VERSE _____
_____
_____
_____

VERSE _____
_____
_____
_____

VERSE _____
_____
_____

MUSIC

Write song structure: VERSE=V, CHORUS=C, BRIDGE=B (V C V C B V C B)

MELODY: write in melody and write chord names above staff lines.

VERSE

CHORUS

BRIDGE

CHORDS:
Write guitar
fingerings used.

SONG TITLE: _____

_____

TEMPO/FEEL: _____

LYRICS

VERSE _____
_____
_____
_____

CHORUS _____
_____
_____
_____

BRIDGE _____
_____
_____
_____

VERSE _____
_____
_____
_____

VERSE _____
_____
_____
_____

VERSE _____
_____
_____

MUSIC

Write song structure: VERSE=V, CHORUS=C, BRIDGE=B (V C V C B V C B)

MELODY: write in melody and write chord names above staff lines.

VERSE

CHORUS

BRIDGE

CHORDS:
Write guitar
fingerings used.

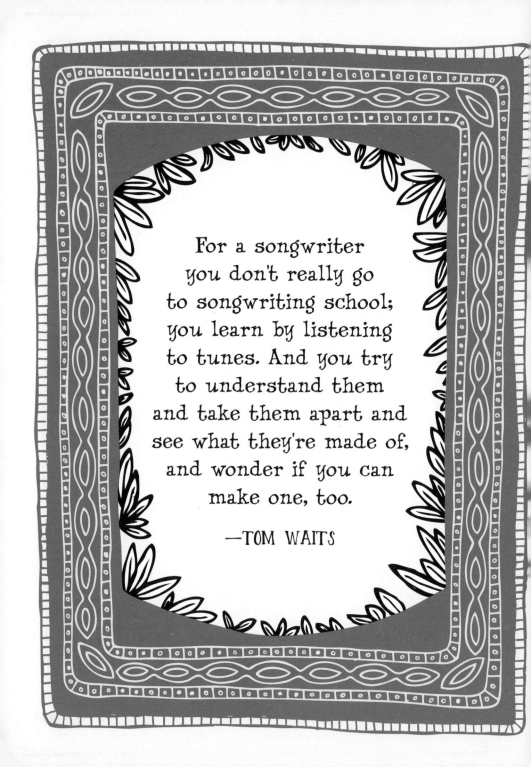

For a songwriter
you don't really go
to songwriting school;
you learn by listening
to tunes. And you try
to understand them
and take them apart and
see what they're made of,
and wonder if you can
make one, too.

—TOM WAITS